AZRIEL RIDES HER MOTORBIKE

By Faith Bin Omar

Library For All Ltd.

DIGITAL EDUCATION

LIBRARY FOR ALL

FOR THE WORLD

Library For All is an Australian not for profit organisation with a mission to make knowledge accessible to all via an innovative digital library solution. Visit us at libraryforall.org

Azriel Rides her Motorbike

First published 2023

Published by Library For All Ltd
Email: info@libraryforall.org
URL: libraryforall.org

Our Yarning logo design by Jason Lee, Bidjipidji Art

Original illustrations by Michael Magpantay

Azriel Rides her Motorbike
Bin Omar, Faith
ISBN: 978-1-922991-20-1
SKU03384

AZRIEL RIDES HER MOTORBIKE

We respect and honour Aboriginal and Torres Strait Islander Elders past, present and future. We acknowledge the stories, traditions and living cultures of Aboriginal and Torres Strait Islander peoples on this land and commit to building a brighter future together.

Azriel is excited to ride
her motorbike near
the flats.

3

She gets all her safety
gear ready to ride,
to be safe.

She puts her helmet, boots, and padded gear on.

She makes sure she tells her parents where she is going.

Azriel loves going fast
on her motorbike.

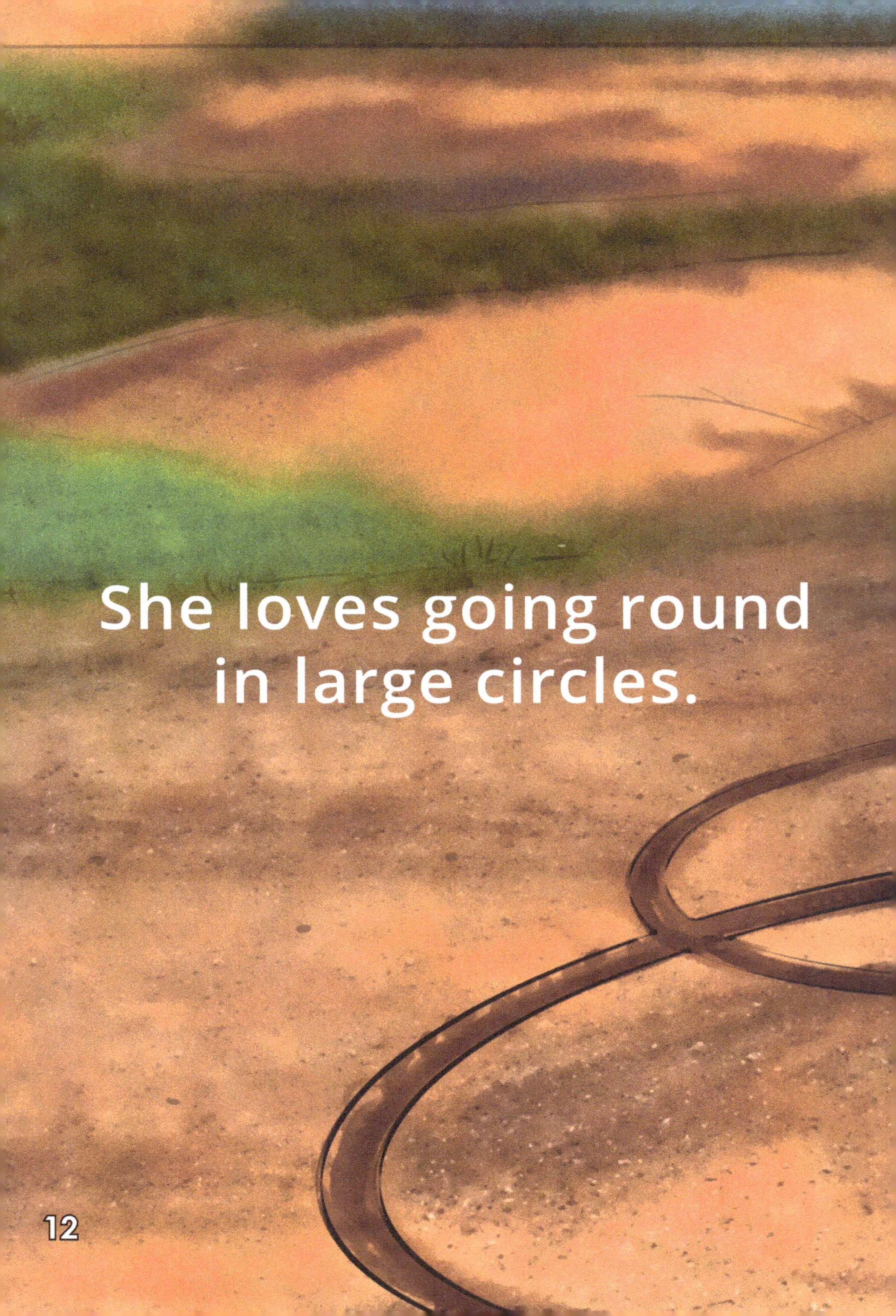

She loves going round in large circles.

She loves going in a
zigzag.

She loves zooming
past trees.

She loves her motorbike and is always careful when she rides it.

You can use these questions to talk about this book with your family, friends and teachers.

What did you learn from this book?

Describe this book in one word. Funny? Scary? Colourful? Interesting?

How did this book make you feel when you finished reading it?

What was your favourite part of this book?

download our reader app
getlibraryforall.org

About the contributors

Faith was born and lives in Derby, Western Australia. She lives with her family, and she loves spending time with them. *Peppa Loves Everyone* was her favourite story when she was a child.

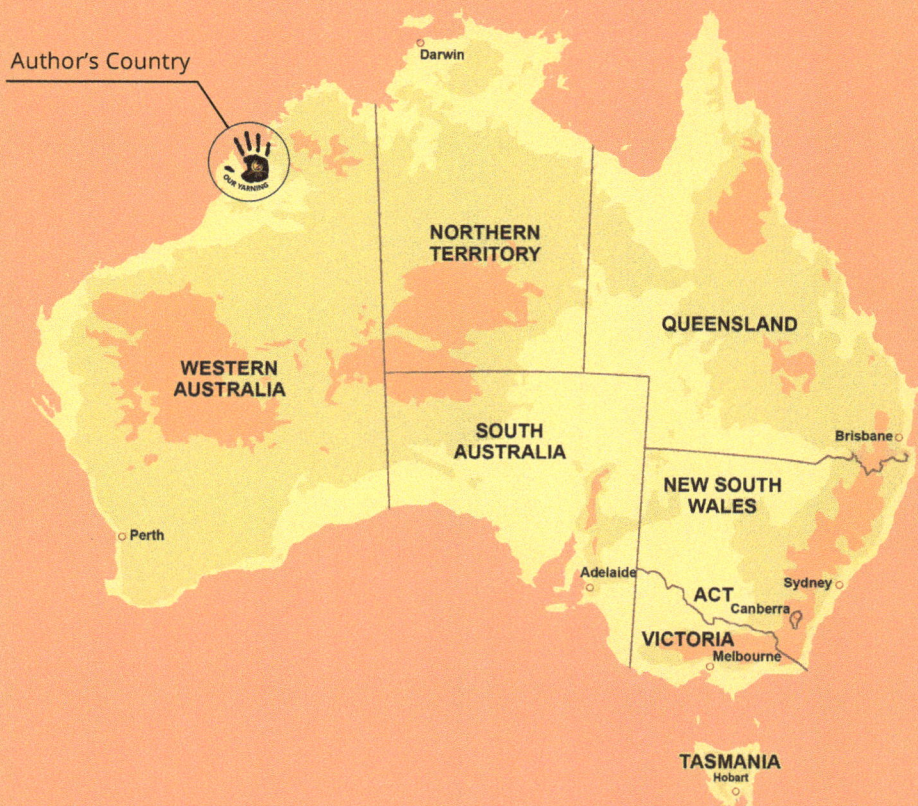

Author's Country

Darwin

NORTHERN
TERRITORY

QUEENSLAND

WESTERN
AUSTRALIA

SOUTH
AUSTRALIA

Brisbane

NEW SOUTH
WALES

Perth

Adelaide

Sydney

ACT
Canberra

VICTORIA

Melbourne

TASMANIA

Hobart

Our Yarning

Want to discover more books from this collection? Our Yarning is a collection of books written by Aboriginal and Torres Strait Islander peoples across Australia.

We know that children learn better, and enjoy reading more, when they see themselves in the stories, characters and illustrations of the books they read.

To download the app, visit the Google Play Store on any Android device and search 'Our Yarning'.

www.ingramcontent.com/pod-product-compliance
Lightning Source LLC
Chambersburg PA
CBHW042346040426
42448CB00019B/3420